Piano · Vocal · Guitar

Best of LITTLE RICHARD

T0101725

Cover Photo Courtesy of Photofest

ISBN-13: 978-1-4234-4927-0
ISBN-10: 1-4234-4927-4

HAL•LEONARD®
CORPORATION

7777 W. BLUEMOUND RD. P.O. BOX 13819 MILWAUKEE, WI 53213

Visit Hal Leonard Online at
www.halleonard.com

BAMA LAMA BAMA LOO

Words and Music by
RICHARD PENNIMAN

GOOD GOLLY MISS MOLLY

Words and Music by ROBERT BLACKWELL
and JOHN MARASCALCO

When you're rock - in' and a -

roll - in', can't hear ___ your mom-ma call.

From the ear - ly, ear - ly morn-in' to the ear - ly, ear - ly night, when I
Mom-ma, Pop - pa told me, "Son, you'd bet - ter watch your step." If they

call Miss Mol - ly's rock - in' at the House of Blue Lights. ___ Good gol - ly Miss
knew a - bout Miss Mol - ly, have to watch my Pop my - self. Go - ing ___ to the

JENNY, JENNY

Words and Music by RICHARD PENNIMAN
and ENOTRIS JOHNSON

Fast Rock & Roll

Jen - ny, Jen - ny, Jen - ny, won't you come a - long with me?

Jen - ny, Jen - ny, woo! Jen - ny, Jen - ny. Jen - ny, Jen - ny, Jen - ny,

won't you come a - long with me? Jen - ny, Jen - ny, woo! Jen - ny, Jen - ny. You

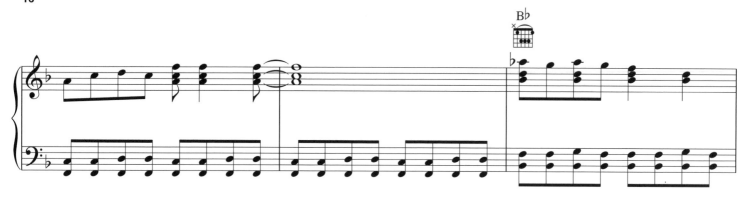

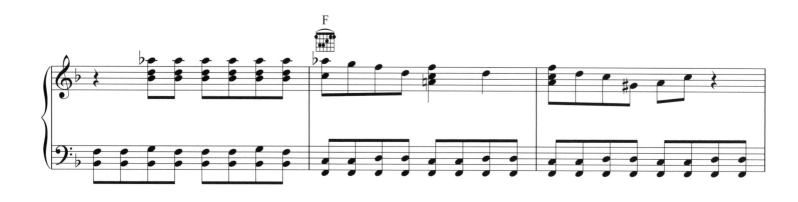

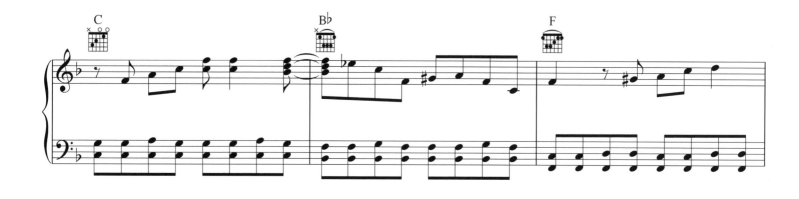

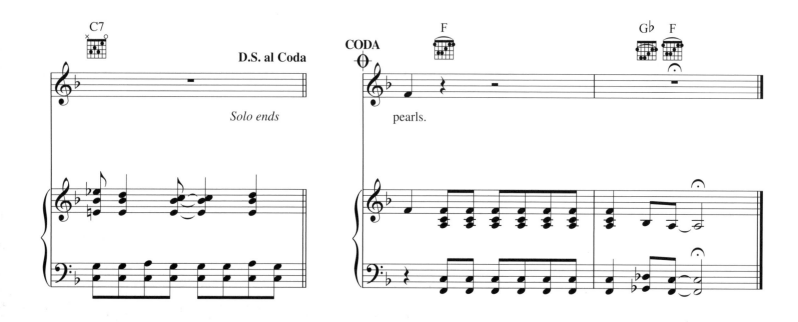

Solo ends

D.S. al Coda

CODA

pearls.

KEEP A-KNOCKIN'

Words and Music by
RICHARD PENNIMAN

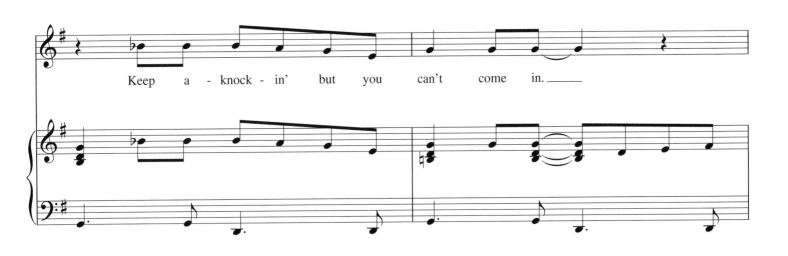

Come back to-mor-row night and try it a-gain.

LONG TALL SALLY

Words and Music by ENOTRIS JOHNSON,
RICHARD PENNIMAN and ROBERT BLACKWELL

Bright Rock

Gon - na tell Aunt Mar - y 'bout Un - cle John; he
Long Tall Sal - ly has a lot on the ball, and
saw Un - cle John with Long Tall ___ Sal - ly; he

says he has the blues, but he has a lot of fun. Oh,
no - bod - y cares if she's long ___ and ___ tall. Oh,
saw Aunt Mar - y com - in' and he ducked back in the al - ley. Oh,

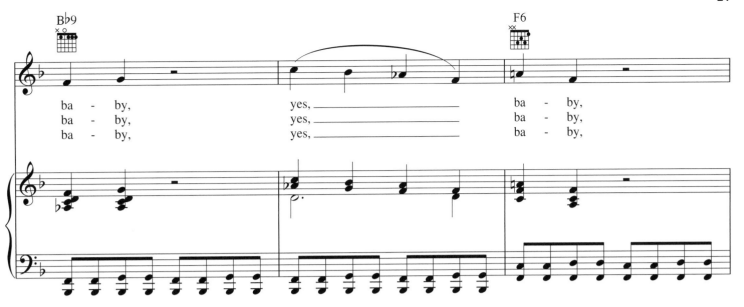

ba - by,   yes, _____ ba - by,
ba - by,   yes, _____ ba - by,
ba - by,   yes, _____ ba - by,

woo, _____ ba - by, _____ hav - in' me some fun to -
woo, _____ ba - by, _____ hav - in' me some fun to -
woo, _____ ba - by, _____ hav - in' me some fun to -

night. ____   Yeah! ____   Well,
night. ____   Well, I
night. ____   Yeah! ____   We're gon - na

LUCILLE
(You Won't Do Your Daddy's Will)

Words and Music by RICHARD PENNIMAN
and ALBERT COLLINS

Medium Boogie

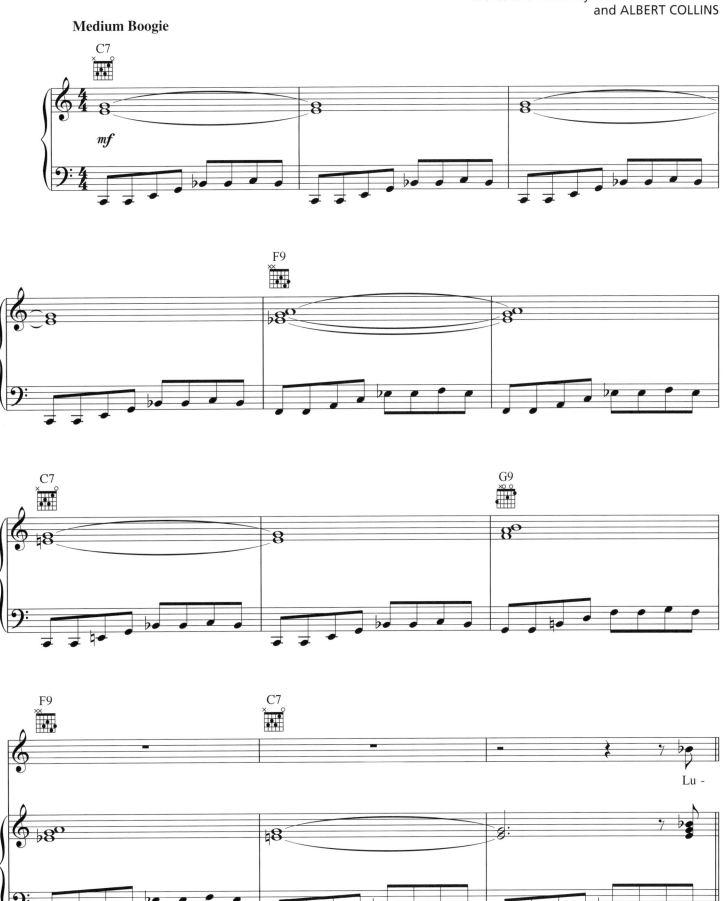

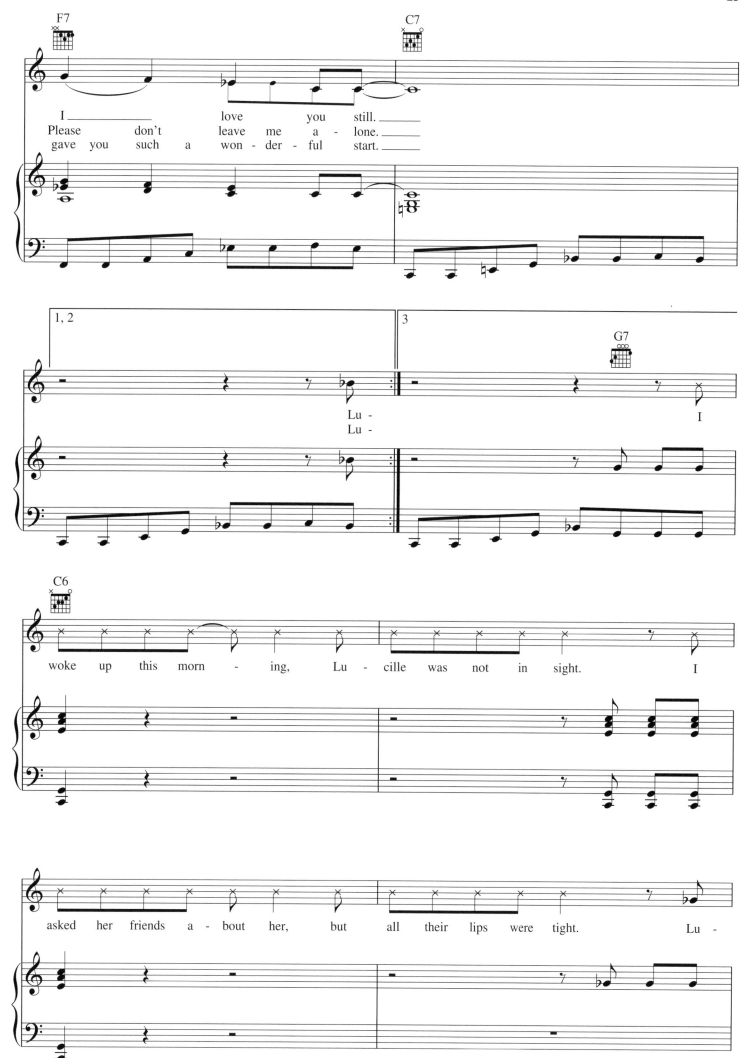

READY TEDDY

Words and Music by JOHN MARASCALCO
and ROBERT BLACKWELL

Bright tempo

Read-y, set, go, man, go, I got a gal that I love so. I'm

read - y read - y read - y Ted - dy. I'm

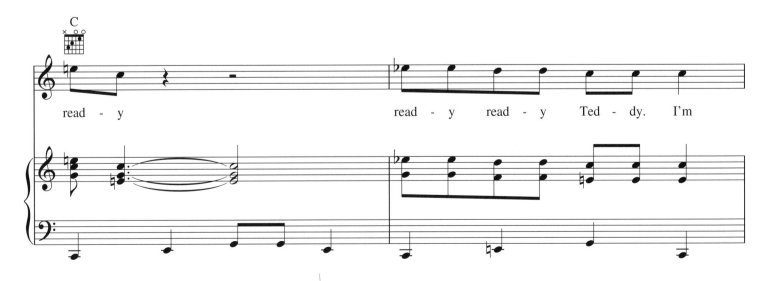

read - y read - y read - y Ted - dy. I'm

OH MY SOUL

Words and Music by
RICHARD PENNIMAN

Recorded a half step higher.

Solo ends

Ba - ba - ba - ba -

ba - by,   don't you know my love is true?_____ Woo!_

SEND ME SOME LOVIN'

Words and Music by JOHN MARASCALCO
and LEO PRICE

RIP IT UP

Words and Music by ROBERT A. BLACKWELL
and JOHN S. MARASCALCO

SLIPPIN' AND SLIDIN'

Words and Music by RICHARD PENNIMAN,
EDWIN BOCAGE, ALBERT COLLINS
and JAMES SMITH

Slip-pin' and a-slid-in', peep-in' and a-hid-in', been told a long time a-
Oh, ___ big con-niv-er, noth-in' but a jiv-er, done got ___ hip to your
Oh, ___ Ma-lin-da, she's a sol-id send-er, you know you bet-ter sur-
Slip-pin' and a-slid-in', peep-in' and a-hid-in', been told a long time a-

TUTTI FRUTTI

Words and Music by LITTLE RICHARD PENNIMAN
and DOROTHY LA BOSTRIE

Bright Rock tempo